EVERYDAY INVENTIONS

AIRPLANES

EVERYDAY INVENTIONS

Kristin Petrie

ABDO Publishing Company

visit us at
www.abdopublishing.com

Published by ABDO Publishing Company, 8000 West 78th Street, Edina, Minnesota 55439.
Copyright © 2009 by Abdo Consulting Group, Inc. International copyrights reserved in all
countries. No part of this book may be reproduced in any form without written permission from the
publisher. The Checkerboard Library™ is a trademark and logo of ABDO Publishing Company.

Printed in the United States.

Cover Photo: Getty Images
Interior Photos: AP Images p. 9; Corbis pp. 10, 11, 20, 25; Getty Images pp. 18, 27, 28, 31;
    iStockphoto pp. 1, 4, 5, 12, 13, 14, 15, 19, 21, 22–23, 24, 25; Lufthansa Cargo p. 29;
    NASA p. 22

Image on pages 16–17 adapted from THE WORLD BOOK ENCYCLOPEDIA. © 2007. By
    permission of the publisher. www.worldbookonline.com

Series Coordinator: Megan M. Gunderson
Editors: Heidi M.D. Elston, Megan M. Gunderson, BreAnn Rumsch
Art Direction & Cover Design: Neil Klinepier

Library of Congress Cataloging-in-Publication Data

Petrie, Kristin, 1970-
  Airplanes / Kristin Petrie.
      p. cm. -- (Everyday inventions)
  Includes bibliographical references and index.
  ISBN 978-1-60453-082-7
  1. Airplanes--Juvenile literature. I. Title.

  TL547.P4229 2009
  629.133'34--dc22

                                        2008001555

CONTENTS

Airplanes

We are all amazed by airplanes. It is almost impossible not to look when one soars above! How do such big, heavy

machines get off the ground? More important, how do they stay in the air?

Have you ever played with an airplane or pretended you were one?

For centuries, people have wanted to fly. This desire probably started simply by watching birds. Soaring high up in the sky, birds have a great view. No traffic jams, rivers, or mountains get in their way. Who wouldn't want to have these same advantages?

People have made many attempts to be human birds. Don't try this at home! Wings and feathers aren't the only things needed to keep you up in the air.

Over the years, airplanes have developed into the speedy machines they are today. They carry mail and people to different countries. And, they deliver many of the products sold in stores. We have many people to thank for the airplanes we see flying today.

Do you want to become a pilot or travel on airplanes to faraway lands?

Timeline

1783	Joseph-Michel and Jacques-Étienne Montgolfier's hot air balloon took flight with human passengers.
1853	Sir George Cayley invented the first glider that could carry a person.
1903	On December 17, Wilbur and Orville Wright flew the first heavier-than-air powered aircraft.
1927	Charles A. Lindbergh flew the first solo, nonstop flight from New York to France.
1932	Amelia Earhart became the first woman to fly solo across the Atlantic Ocean.
1957	By this year, more people were crossing the Atlantic Ocean by airplane than by ship.
1986	Dick Rutan and Jeana Yeager became the first people to fly around the world without stopping or refueling.

Airplane Facts

○ What are the mysterious black boxes people search for after an airplane crashes? They are data recorders. One kind tracks data such as an airplane's speed, direction, and altitude. Another kind records voices and other noises in the cockpit. In case of a crash, this information can help determine the causes that led to the accident.

○ An automatic flight control system is better known as autopilot. Autopilot allows an airplane to fly using a combination of sensors and computer programs. Together, these determine and adjust an airplane's speed, direction, altitude, and other important functions. Autopilot means less work for a pilot during normal flight. It also assists a pilot flying or landing in difficult conditions.

○ To fly for a U.S. airline, pilots must have a commercial pilot license and an airline transport pilot license from the Federal Aviation Administration (FAA). They must be at least 23 years old and pass physical, written, and flight tests. And, they must have completed at least 1,500 hours of flight time.

First in Flight

In the late 1400s, Leonardo da Vinci became one of the first people to study flight. He did this by observing the wings, tails, and feathers of birds. Leonardo was fascinated by these marvelous creatures.

After studying birds, Leonardo illustrated an idea for a flying machine called an ornithopter. This aircraft was designed to be powered by a person flapping wings attached to his arms. The invention looked similar to a modern airplane, but it did not work. Leonardo also designed a kind of helicopter and a parachute.

Hundreds of years later, French brothers Joseph-Michel and Jacques-Étienne Montgolfier created balloons filled with hot air. On November 21, 1783, Frenchmen Jean-François Pilâtre de Rozier and François d'Arlandes ascended in a Montgolfier balloon. This was the first human flight in an aircraft that was not attached to the ground.

From 1891 to 1896, Otto Lilienthal made more than 2,000 glider flights. He flew 1,150 feet (350 m) on his longest flight. Lilienthal died in 1896 after a glider crash.

Then in 1853, scientist Sir George Cayley invented the first man-carrying glider. German engineer Otto Lilienthal improved on the heavier-than-air glider. His aircraft could be piloted and could carry a person for greater distances. Lilienthal also wrote one of the first books on **aeronautics**.

In the late 1800s, Orville and Wilbur Wright studied Lilienthal's theories. Then, they began inventing and testing heavier-than-air powered aircraft. The Wright brothers used a gasoline engine in their flying machine.

After his success, Charles A. Lindbergh continued working with airplanes. He flew all over the world charting new airline routes.

The first flight was on December 17, 1903. The airplane traveled 120 feet (37 m). This long-awaited first flight lasted 12 seconds. By the final flight of this historic day, the craft flew 852 feet (260 m) in just under one minute.

After this success, the science of flight advanced quickly. By the 1920s, airplanes could fly much farther. In 1927, Charles A. Lindbergh flew the *Spirit of St. Louis* nonstop from an airfield near New York City, New York, to one near Paris, France. It was the world's first solo flight across the Atlantic Ocean.

In 1937, Amelia Earhart attempted to fly around the world. She disappeared over the Pacific Ocean on July 2.

In 1932, Amelia Earhart became the first woman to fly this course alone. Lindbergh's Atlantic flight had taken 33 hours and 30 minutes. But Earhart made the trip from Harbour Grace, Newfoundland, Canada, to Londonderry, Northern Ireland, in a record-breaking 14 hours and 56 minutes!

Throughout the 1900s, military groups used airplanes extensively and numerous records were broken. By 1957, more people were crossing the Atlantic Ocean by airplane than by ship. Then in 1986, Dick Rutan and Jeana Yeager became the first people to fly around the world without stopping or refueling. Today, computers are helping people design aircraft that are faster and larger than ever before.

Bits and Pieces

The fuselage of smaller airplanes may hold the pilot and a few passengers in the same area. But larger airplanes have a separate cabin that may hold more than 550 passengers!

What part of an airplane amazes you? For many, it is the body because it can be so large. The body, or fuselage, of most airplanes has a big job. It holds everything in, including people and cargo. It is also the anchor for the wings, the tail, and the landing gear.

The wings may be the most important part of an airplane. Without them, an airplane cannot fly! Wings have moving parts called ailerons. An aileron is located at the trailing edge of each side of an airplane wing. Ailerons work in opposite directions to allow the airplane to **bank** for turns. When the right aileron is up, the left aileron is down. This causes the airplane to bank right.

Many airplane wings also have flaps hinged to them.
These are located close to the fuselage on the wing's trailing
edge. When lowered, the flaps help the
airplane take off. The flaps can also be used
to help an airplane slow down.

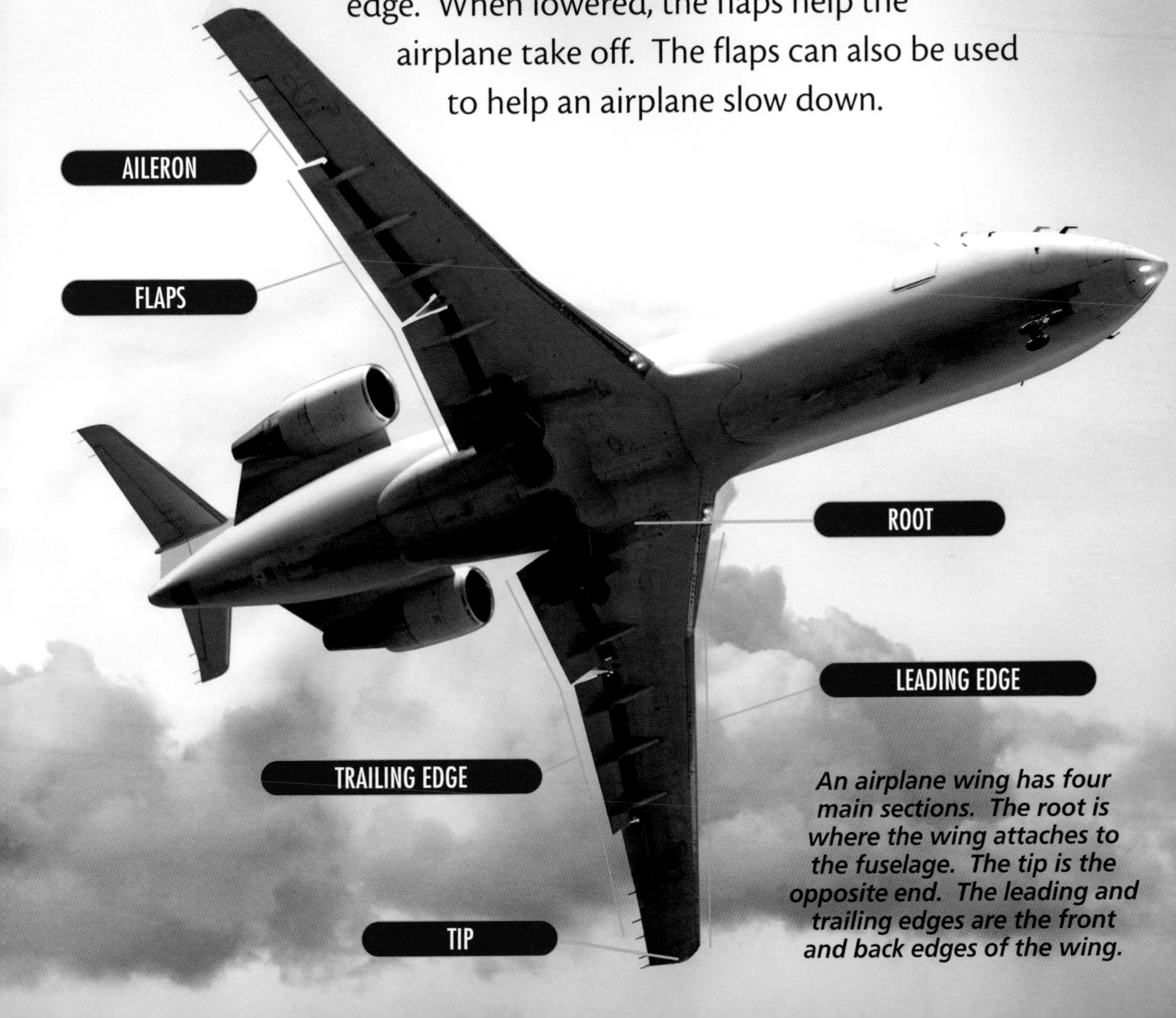

AILERON

FLAPS

ROOT

LEADING EDGE

TRAILING EDGE

An airplane wing has four main sections. The root is where the wing attaches to the fuselage. The tip is the opposite end. The leading and trailing edges are the front and back edges of the wing.

TIP

What else does an airplane need? How about landing gear! An airplane's wheels are vital for takeoff and landing. Most larger airplanes have retractable landing gear. This means the wheels are drawn into the body during flight. Pulling the landing gear into the body makes the airplane more **streamlined** while in flight.

Next is the tail. An airplane's tail has two winglike parts. They project up and out from the back of the body. The first part is the tail fin. The second part is the horizontal stabilizer. Together, these parts help keep an airplane flying straight.

Both the tail fin and the horizontal stabilizer have moving parts controlled by the pilot. On the tail fin, the rudder is the moving part. The rudder keeps

Tricycle landing gear

Tail-wheel landing gear

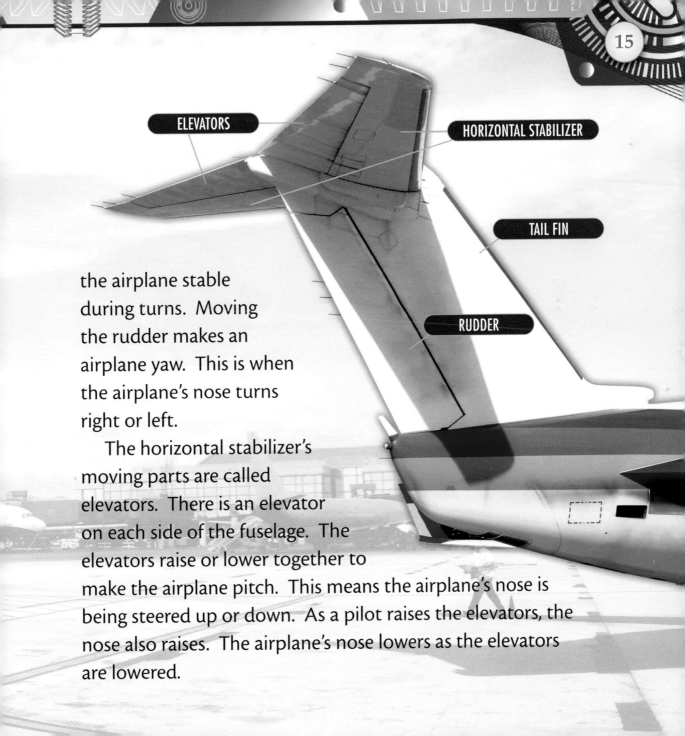

ELEVATORS

HORIZONTAL STABILIZER

TAIL FIN

RUDDER

the airplane stable during turns. Moving the rudder makes an airplane yaw. This is when the airplane's nose turns right or left.

The horizontal stabilizer's moving parts are called elevators. There is an elevator on each side of the fuselage. The elevators raise or lower together to make the airplane pitch. This means the airplane's nose is being steered up or down. As a pilot raises the elevators, the nose also raises. The airplane's nose lowers as the elevators are lowered.

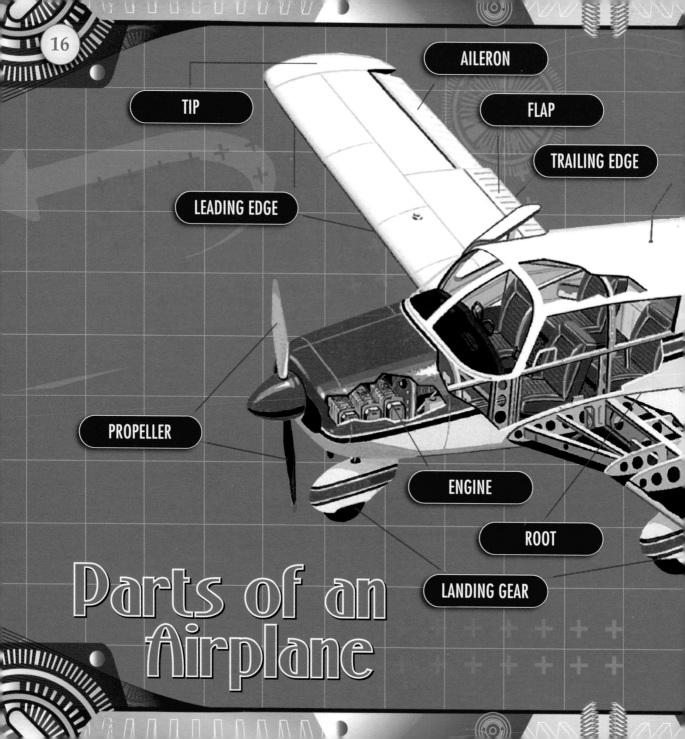

AILERON

FLAP

TRAILING EDGE

TIP

LEADING EDGE

PROPELLER

ENGINE

ROOT

LANDING GEAR

Parts of an Airplane

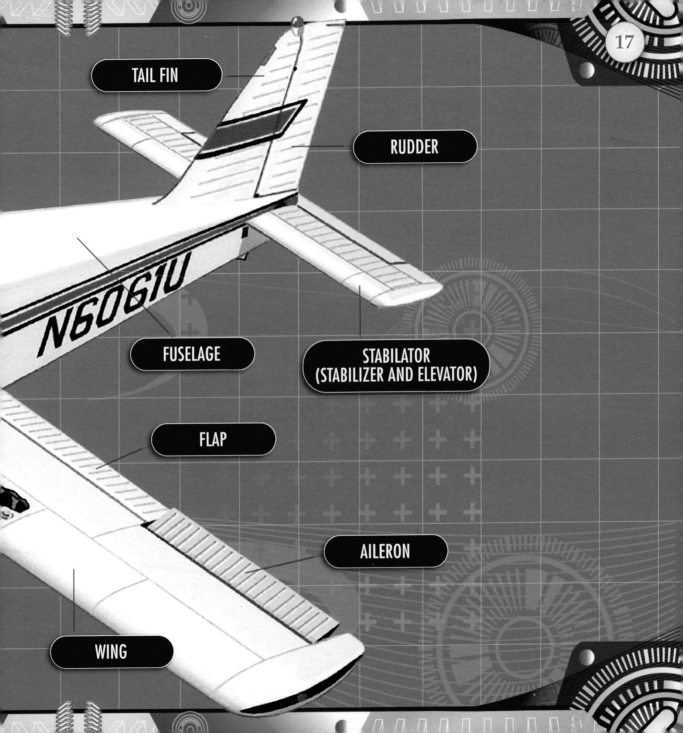

TAIL FIN

RUDDER

N6061U

FUSELAGE

STABILATOR
(STABILIZER AND ELEVATOR)

FLAP

AILERON

WING

Power Sources

Pilots depend on an array of instruments to fly safely from one location to the next.

In the **cockpit**, pilots use various controls and instruments to fly an airplane. A yoke controls ailerons and elevators. Rudder pedals move the rudder from side to side. Flight instruments show speed and altitude. Engine instruments display such things as fuel supply.

An airplane's power comes from its engine. There are three main types of airplane engines. These are reciprocating, jet, and rocket engines.

Reciprocating engines power airplanes equipped with propellers. A propeller may look like a household fan. But, the engine turns the propeller quickly to move an airplane forward through the air. Single-engine airplanes usually have a propeller on the aircraft's nose. Airplanes with more than one engine usually have propellers attached to their wings.

Aircraft with jet engines are faster and more powerful than those with reciprocating engines. Jet engines take in air and burn it with fuel to form **exhaust**. The escaping exhaust spins a **turbine**, which powers the engine. Rocket engines operate at high speeds and are expensive. So, they are used mostly in test airplanes and military aircraft.

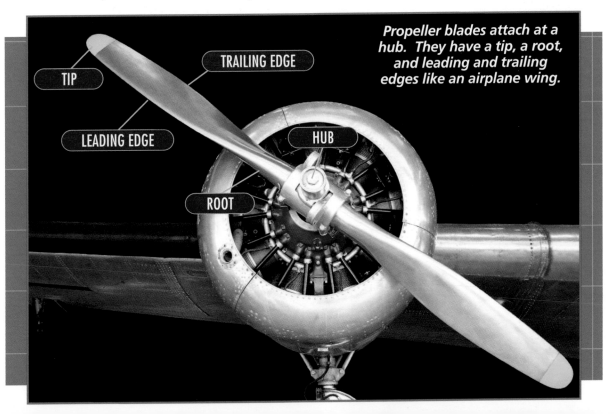

Propeller blades attach at a hub. They have a tip, a root, and leading and trailing edges like an airplane wing.

TRAILING EDGE

TIP

LEADING EDGE

HUB

ROOT

External Forces

Airplanes are carefully designed machines. Their **streamlined** shape allows air to lift them and keep them up. That's right, the same air that messes up your hair helps lift an airplane!

Airplane wings are curved. Their shape catches lots of air under the wing. This causes more air to push up on the wing than down. Air flows faster over a wing than under it. And, a wing pushes air downward as it moves forward. All together, that means the airplane moves upward. This is called lift.

Lift keeps the airplane up. Luckily, another force keeps it from rocketing up into outer space! This force is gravity. Gravity and lift work together to keep the airplane level in the air.

Ice affects an airplane's wing shape. This changes how well an airplane flies. Deicing fluid removes ice and prevents it from forming.

LIFT

AIRFLOW

The design and shape of an airplane wing affect airflow and make lift possible.

Two other forces keep the airplane moving forward, but not too fast. These are drag and thrust. Drag pulls the airplane back. You feel drag when you walk into the wind. Thrust is what keeps air cruising past an airplane's wings.

Propellers and engines create thrust to move the airplane forward. Using a propeller to create thrust is like producing lift sideways. A spinning propeller has more air pressure behind it than in front of it. This pushes the airplane forward.

THRUST - Propellers and engines create thrust to pull an airplane through the air. It works against drag and makes lift possible.

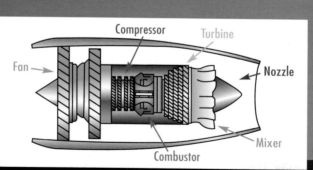

Fan → | Compressor | Turbine | Nozzle | Mixer | Combustor

JET ENGINES

Turbojet engines take in air and burn it with fuel. This produces exhaust, which spins the turbine and also creates thrust. Turbofan engines *(above)* are more powerful than turbojets. This is because a fan at the front of the engine takes in more air. Turboprops are turbojet engines with a propeller.

A jet engine takes in air to create thrust. This air is **compressed**. Then, it moves back into the engine's combustion chamber. There, compressed air burns with fuel to create **exhaust**. Exhaust leaves the engine at a high speed. This pushes the engine forward and creates thrust.

LIFT - As an airplane moves forward, air flowing over and under its wing keeps the airplane up. It works against gravity.

DRAG - An airplane's streamlined design reduces the forces of air pushing against it as it moves.

GRAVITY - An airplane's weight naturally pulls it toward the ground.

Regimes of Flight

Airplanes are organized by the jobs they perform, such as general, commercial, or military aviation. And, airplanes are sorted into a regime of flight by the speed at which they travel. Regimes of flight are categorized by **Mach number**.

Subsonic aircraft travel slower than Mach 1, which is the speed of sound. Depending on altitude, this is around 761 miles per hour (1,225 km/hr). Most commercial jets are subsonic.

Transonic aircraft travel between Mach .9 and Mach 1.4. Any airplane traveling faster than the speed of sound is considered supersonic. Hypersonic aircraft travel more than five times the speed of sound, or Mach 5.

Biplane

Aircraft are also grouped by the number of wings they have. Monoplanes have one continuous wing. Biplanes have two wings on each side of the fuselage, one above the other.

Floatplane

Glider

Floatplanes and flying boats are built to take off of and land on water! Instead of using wheels as landing gear, floatplanes have floats. Flying boats have smooth, boatlike bottoms.

A glider, or sailplane, is similar to an airplane. But, it has no engine. Gliders use air currents and **updrafts** to stay in the air. They were invented before modern powered airplanes. But, they are still popular today!

A Team Effort

Not just anyone can fly an airplane. To operate aircraft, a person must be a **certified** pilot. On commercial airplanes, there are at least two pilots. The captain is the pilot in charge. He or she flies the airplane and directs the crew.

The second pilot is called the copilot or first officer. The first officer has his or her own set of controls. This person and the captain take turns flying the airplane. The first officer also helps the captain with other important duties before and during the flight.

Sometimes, a third person works in the **cockpit**. He or she is called the second officer or the flight engineer. The flight engineer's job is to **monitor** the airplane's systems. But today, many of these systems are monitored by computers.

Flight attendants have an important job. They are trained to keep things running smoothly in both everyday and emergency situations. They continually ensure that passengers are safe and comfortable.

Flight attendants serve food and beverages and help people safely store their luggage.

While you are finding your airplane seat, the ground crew is hard at work. The ground crew has a variety of jobs, including loading luggage. **Maintenance crews** help keep airplanes running smoothly.

Even more people work inside the airport. Staff members check luggage for safety and weight. Security guards ensure the safety of everyone wishing to fly. At the control tower, someone arranges each takeoff and landing. Still others are planning each airplane's next adventure.

A Small World

Whew! That's a lot to think about. After all, airplanes have a big impact on our world. For starters, airplanes get us to different places quickly. In 1492, Christopher Columbus spent more than a month sailing across the Atlantic Ocean. Today, you can make that trip in less than seven hours on an airplane!

Airplanes are an important means of transportation for businesspeople, for vacationers, and even for your mail!

Did someone in your house get mail today? Those letters came from different locations. Many traveled by airplane. Now, look in the kitchen. Is there fruit? How about seafood? These foods may have come from another state, or even another country. Thanks to airplanes, we enjoy fresh food from around the world.

Airplanes have allowed different nations to open up to one another. Unfortunately, disease and illness spread more quickly with this fast form of transportation. And, jet engines create noise and air pollution. Hopefully, many of these negative effects will be improved in the future. That way, airplanes will continue to make positive contributions to our everyday lives.

Some commercial airplanes transport both passengers and cargo. Others transport only cargo.

GLOSSARY

aeronautics (ehr-uh-NAW-tihks) - a science dealing with the design, manufacture, and operation of aircraft.

bank - to tilt an airplane to one side or the other, especially when turning.

certify - to recognize that a person or a thing has met specific requirements.

cockpit - the area where a pilot and a copilot sit to fly an airplane.

compress - to squeeze together and reduce in size, especially to make fit in a smaller space.

exhaust - used gas or vapor that escapes from an engine.

Mach number - a number showing the relationship of an airplane's speed to the speed of sound. An aircraft moving at the speed of sound has a Mach number of one.

maintenance crew - a group of people in charge of the upkeep, such as repairing and cleaning, of something.

monitor - to watch, keep track of, or oversee.

streamlined - designed to reduce drag or resistance to motion when moving through air or water.

turbine - a device with rotating blades that are turned by a moving force, such as water, steam, gas, or wind. A turbine turns the energy of movement into mechanical power.

updraft - an upward movement of a gas, such as air.

WEB SITES

To learn more about airplanes, visit ABDO Publishing Company on the World Wide Web at www.abdopublishing.com. Web sites about airplanes are featured on our Book Links page. These links are routinely monitored and updated to provide the most current information available.

INDEX

A
ailerons 12, 18
Arlandes, François d' 8
Atlantic Ocean 10, 11, 28

B
biplanes 24

C
Cayley, George 9
cockpit 18, 26
Columbus, Christopher 28
crew 26, 27

D
drag 22

E
Earhart, Amelia 11
elevators 15, 18
engines 10, 18, 19, 22, 23, 25, 29

F
flaps 13
floatplanes 25
flying boats 25
fuel 11, 18, 19, 23
fuselage 12, 13, 14, 15, 24

G
gliders 9, 25
gravity 20

H
horizontal stabilizer 14, 15
hot air balloons 8

L
landing gear 12, 14, 25
Leonardo da Vinci 8
lift 20, 22
Lilienthal, Otto 9, 10
Lindbergh, Charles A. 10, 11

M
monoplanes 24
Montgolfier, Jacques-Étienne 8
Montgolfier, Joseph-Michel 8

O
ornithopter 8

P
Pilâtre de Rozier, Jean-François 8
pilots 14, 15, 18, 26
propellers 18, 19, 22

R
regimes of flight 24
rudder 14, 15, 18
Rutan, Dick 11

T
tail 12, 14
tail fin 14
thrust 22, 23

W
wings 12, 13, 19, 20, 22, 24
Wright, Orville 10
Wright, Wilbur 10

Y
Yeager, Jeana 11